This is a bucket list item...so don't expect anything profound!

D. Shanee

BookLeaf Publishing

India | USA | UK

Presentation by *BookLeaf Publishing*

Web: www.bookleafpub.com

E-mail: info@bookleafpub.com

ISBN: 9789363314818

First edition 2024

"Hand in hand we come

Christopher Robin and I

To lay this book in your lap.

Say you're surprised?

Say you like it?

Say it's just what you wanted?

Because it's yours-

because we love you."

— A.A. Milne, Winnie-the-Pooh

PREFACE

This book of poems, thoughts, and feelings is my surprise gift to those I love. Perhaps you'll understand me a little better. Perhaps you won't.

I never intended anything within this book to be disclosed to the masses. I wrote things simply for self-perseverance. By publishing them, I am killing two bucket list items at once: write a book and brag that I am a "published author".

Please don't try to make sense of anything or "read between the lines" on things that you read or else you are sure to be disappointed. Sorry. I'm not that deep. Enjoy it for what it is.

Do you hear me, Universe?!?

They say what you profess
is what you possess,
well, that explains why I'm so tired and stressed!
When stating intent, be concise and clear.
Speak boldly and loudly so the "Universe"
hears.

Don't speak upon what ifs, maybes, what could
be,
what may or may not, what sounds like it should
be.
Unintentional deceit makes many of us "try-ers"
you either do or you don't, so "try-ers" are liars!

Ask for what you want, what you need and
deserve,
bold accomplishments and results- no request is
too absurd!
Speak with conviction for we are what we say,
we are what we think and what our actions
convey.

I want comfort and peace, love, forgiveness,
stronger mental health, invest more in my
fitness,

success for my children and all of my heirs,
may they be happy and healthy, mentally strong,
and self-aware!

I want outstanding communication, a refreshed
outlook on life,
marital bliss, travel, to become a trophy wife.
A completely healthy family, wealth, education
Business success, happiness, consideration.

A comfortable retirement, money saved in
abundance,
new exciting ideas- no repeats, no redundance!
Publish a book, start a memorial fund,
A girls trip in the tropics, register to carry a
concealed gun.

Do something spontaneous, something insane,
drive to the airport and hop on the next plane!
Walk into a store and buy everyone's things,
learn to play the piano and learn how to sing.

They say what you profess
is what you possess,
that explains why I'll no longer be tired or
stressed.
I've stated intent. I've been concise and clear.
I spoke boldly and loudly so the "Universe"
could hear.

January 21, 2023

Like a breath of crisp air on a cold morning,
without warning,
a verbal shock was delivered to my system.
I sat in disbelief.
Unable to discern, process or comprehend
such vile words.
I scanned the room looking for any sign or clue
to let me know this was a nightmare or a twisted
prank phone call.
It wasn't.
My watery eyes locked with hers.
This was new to her.
She had never seen her mother react this way to
ANYTHING.
 I broke our gaze and turned away, but it was too
late.
Her tears had already begun to flow as she
clutched her baby and rocked back and forth.
"Don't look at her!", I told myself as I exited the
living room and paced back and forth beside the
kitchen island clutching the phone to my ear.
"You'll call back in 5 minutes? Okay."

*Insert the longest 5 minutes of my life.
Repeating the phone call multiple times. A

breakdown in my husband's arms. A phone call
to an auntie. Hoping. Praying.*

"What if? Nah. No way. She's okay. She's gonna
be fine. They're gonna tell me that she's now
responsive."
The phone finally rings again.
"Ma'am....", I was snapped back to reality by the
doctor's monotone voice.
"This is doctor
whogivesashitwhathernamewas. We called her
death at 11:51pm. I'm so sorry."
I was instantly filled with rage, anger, sorrow,
sadness, hurt, regret, frustration, guilt, pain,
skepticism, distress, weakness and loss.
I finally allowed the tears to flow openly and
freely down my cheeks.
All I could muster was the word "Okay".
O-fuckin-kay.

What a Beautiful Day

I sit in dismal silence.
Viewing the beauty from within.
The sun is beaming down on the earth like the
flickering flame of a campfire...
beautiful and warm.
I smile as I taste the freshness of the air.
The burden on my shoulders has been lifted.
The smell of the thought of such beauty entices
me.
I am a human sponge absorbing all that I
encounter on this beautiful day.

Grieve

I'm grieving the rose-colored glasses that I chose to see you through.
I'm grieving the frustration and pain of what I feel was an avoidable death.
I'm grieving the regret that I've felt for not always being there for you. Where was I during the most monumental events in your life?!?
I'm grieving the fact that we were strangers to the intimacies of each other's lives.
I'm grieving the biggest loss of my life.
My Mother.
My Mom.
My Mommy.
I'm grieving for a friend that I miss dearly.
I'm grieving the loss of a mentor, a supporter, a counselor.
I'm grieving what I've come to realize is my reflection.

I See Nothing Has Changed (2010ish)

I'd do anything for you! For you I'd die.
But the real question is, would you continue
with life?
Would you push to the side false beliefs and
self-doubt,
The self-sabotage, stress, self-harm and burn
out?
Would you move yourself up to the top spot on
your list?
Give yourself mercy, grace, self-love,
forgiveness?
Hmmm…I'm not sure but I think I can try.
You're so full of shit, girl you know that's a lie!
Stop filling your head with false thoughts and
delusions!
It leads to depression, anxiety, seclusion.
I need you to treat me the way you treat THEM,
You put then at the top…there the" crème de la
crème!"
You listen with love and then give great advice,
if they need anything you don't even think
twice!
You open your purse or your heart and you pour
into those that you respect, like, love, and adore.

But you always leave out the most important
person,
to her you lie, steal, create elaborate diversions.
You talk to her crazy without much regard-
no wonder she constantly has up her guard!
Please choose your words wisely for she hears
them clearly.
She rarely hears praise so she clings to them
dearly!
She's battling inner demons who beg, steal and
cheat,
They win every time- she's in constant defeat.
I need you to do better, please value your space.
Be patient, be kind, to yourself extend grace.
It takes lots of time to unlearn these things,
Like a cocoon converts to a butterfly with wings,
I want better for you!
-So do I, so do I!
Then start living for "yourself"- stop with the
"try's."

The Collector

I watch the excitement in your eyes when the
hunt is on.
It's all about the thrill of the chase.
Bragging rights.
To be able to say that you were the first to have
it
or
yours is newer and better than theirs, appears to
be the goal.
But what happens when the "newness" wears
off?
Is it still invaluable to you?
Is it time for an upgrade?
Can you ever truly be satisfied if you're
constantly looking for the next, best thing?

I wonder.....

We Are What We Behold

Your smile illuminates the darkest corners of my
soul.
I love to sit and watch as your curiosity is
piqued, and you explore new concepts and
environments.
Your discoveries typically lead to a newly
learned skill or word.
I watch as you squeal in 90 decibel excitement.
Hearing your voice and your laughter dissolves
any and all of the hurt and pain that I carry.
Your gentle hugs and 'mooches radiate
throughout my body, absorbing and
overpowering the darkness while invigorating
new life into me.
You arrived in God's perfect timing…ready to
rescue me from life's devastation.
Is it possible to be a reincarnation of someone
who is alive…but on their way to the other side?
Because your reflection is her reflection. Your
disposition is her disposition. Your quirkiness is
her quirkiness.
No, you say? Hmmm.
Well, they say when God wants something done,
he sends a child.

God sent THIS child into my world to provide love, peace, and comfort in the times to come; and I have to tell you that I have never been more grateful for a gift.
The bible says, "A pleasant thing it is for the eyes to behold the sun. To behold the sun is to enjoy life; for light, which is life, is derived from the sun."
We are what we behold.

Dear God

I just want to take a moment to Thank you for all the blessings in my life.
Thank you for allowing me to wake up this morning. I understand that is a privilege and a very special gift from you.
Thank you for the love and comfort of my family.
Thank you for the gift of partnership with my husband. I pray your abundant blessings over his life, his work, and every aspect of his life.
Thank you for allowing the 5 suns in my life to rise each morning. I am grateful for these "sunrises" that bring hope, peace, and joy into each and every one of my days!
Thank you for your guidance and your hedge of protection around all of that I love.
Thank you for never abandoning me…even when it appears that I have abandoned you.
I repent of focusing on the things (and people) that I don't have, instead of focusing on the blessings You have provided for myself, family, friends and loved ones.
Please forgive me for overlooking Your presence in every aspect of my life.

Forgive me for the ways I fall short. I beg for
your forgiveness.
Thank you for providing me with resilience,
understanding, strength and resources to
navigate the storm that I endured in 2023.
Thank you for providing comfort and peace in
my times of sorrow and distress. I ask that you
please heal my emotional wounds and replace
them with whatever you feel I am lacking.
Please surround me with positive and supportive
family, friends, and influences.
Lord, I pray that I draw closer to you and that
my understanding of your Word and wisdom
deepens. Help me to strengthen my relationship
with you so that it may become the foundation
of my life. I ask that you help me to align my
thoughts and beliefs with yours so that they
reflect each other. I ask for a renewal of faith,
hope, and forgiveness.
I ask and speak these things in your name.
I give you all the honor, all the praise, and all the
glory.
In your beautiful, majestic name I pray,
AMEN

Thought-Expectations of the SBW

Being labeled a "strong, black woman" is often more damaging than it is endearing. Although most think it's a term of endearment, it is actually a burden to feel like we have to be "superwomen" all of the time.

It places unnecessary stress and pressure on our already loaded shoulders. We wear this armor, this title, like a badge of honor. But is it?

Why must we feel obligated to constantly self-sacrifice, suppress our feelings and emotions, resist vulnerability, present an image of brutal emotional and mental strength and have a strong obligation to help others?

No other race of women has the pressure or expectation to survive it all, to withstand EVERYTHING thrown at them, and to often suffer in silence...and be proud of doing so.

Is this a blessing or a curse? Maybe we want to be "saved" too.

New Me? Who dis?

Emotionally numb.
Words disappear from the tip of my tongue.
At a loss for words to speak
Fatigued, tired and weak.
Hunger dissipates.
Weight fluctuates.
Tears have dried out.
I'm all cried out.
Maneuvering the world on autopilot
Tunnel vision.
Newly gained inhibition
Social life a distant memory
Feels like friends have abandoned me.
Maybe I have abandoned them?
Insomnia has set in.
Damn.

Mac Blade

Maybe we should've...kept in touch more
frequently.
Maybe we could've...been closer than we were.
What would've happened if we...both put forth
the maximum effort to make things work?
Whatever.
It was what it was.
It, now, is what it is with no chance of righting
our wrongs.
Know that I loved you.
Know that I miss you.
Oddly enough, your demise created a new bond.
The six of us are now accountable to and for
each other.
And for that I am grateful.
Continue to Rest in Love and Light.

Control Top (2005ish)

Do you hold yourself together like control top
pantyhose?
Suck it up.
Suck it in.
Squeeze tight with all your might.

You look good.
On the outside.
But on the inside your struggling to breathe.
Held together under the false pretense of vanity.
It's insanity.

You're perfectly smooth.
Not an atom out of place.
The silhouette of Josephine or Eartha-
hips wide, bust full.
Silky, compressed.

Below, you're on the verge of explosion.
Bubbly. Oozing. Lack of circulation.
It hurts.
So, we suffer in silence rather than expose
ourselves to the masses.
With our fat asses.

Life Without You

Mom,

I need you to know that:

-My hurt is deep and loud, but my faith and my God are so much louder. I'm going to be okay.
-A part of me is still missing and I wonder if I will ever get it back. Maybe that piece...or peace...is with you in Heaven and will remain there until I arrive too.
-You appear so vividly in my dreams that I am often tricked into thinking it is real. Waking up in sorrow and realizing that it was a dream is gut-wrenching and the hardest part of those days.
-Talking about you is cathartic for me yet heartbreaking. You left such a huge mark in this world and were respected and loved by many. Smiles, laughter, and tears are common responses to stories about you.
-I feel like I'm waiting. I'm waiting for you to call and tell me that the past year was a really elaborate bad joke. I'm waiting for you to call and gossip with me. I'm waiting for you to send a card in the mail. I'm waiting for you to tell me

all about the concert you just went to. I'm
waiting for you to tell me how much you won at
bingo. Waiting. I'm constantly waiting.
-Each time that I walk into your house is like
playing Russian roulette with my emotions.
Some visits I am proud of the progress that has
been made and think that you would be proud as
well. Other times I am sad because I am slowly
erasing what's left of your physical presence in
this world.
-I only ever made one promise to you that I
intend to keep. You know what it is.
You'll have a front row seat from Heaven. I hope
you'll cheer loudly when the time comes.
-I miss you. I miss your smile that you always
concealed in pictures, your voice, your loud
cackle of a laugh, your hugs. I look for you in
everything that I do. I wait for your signs when
making decisions. You always make your
presence felt but I still miss your physical form.
I forever will.
-All I have left are smile-less pictures (which is
ironic because you were ALWAYS laughing,
smiling, and joking) and memories. I wish you
would have smiled more because the pictures
don't depict the life, adventures, and experiences
that you truly lived. I guess that's where the
memories come in.

-I smile when I think of all the beautiful memories that we created...and then I am reminded that you are no longer here. When my memory starts to fail me, and I only have pictures, I pray that I remember the "true" you. I will forever treasure the memories and hold them dear.

-I have guilt and regret. Where was I during the most important times in your life? Why wasn't I there? Why didn't I ask more questions or "dig deeper" when your responses were vague? The realization that I wasn't there for you the way I should have been is worse than the pain of your death and will forever haunt me. I'm sorry.

-Your death was a brutal lesson to many about the arrogance of time. "I don't have time for all of that" "I'll do it tomorrow" "I'll wait it out and if I still don't feel good, I'll make an appointment". I wish the universe presented this lesson in another way.

-I always looked at you as "superwoman". I never saw you stressed out. I never saw you worry. I never saw you overly emotional and I never saw you shed a tear. I subconsciously molded myself around your example. I now know why. One day I would need your superhuman type strength to bear your loss.

-The bottom line is that I miss you like crazy, mom. We weren't perfect but we were a good team. Some day we will reunite in Heaven and catch up over a cup of tea. In the meantime, I hope that you will continue to guide, watch, and protect me/us from Heaven. I love you.

To You Sir, With Love

You.
It's you.
It's always you.
It's always been you.
It will always be you. Forever.
You will forever be ... my choice.
My everything.
My prayer.
My Love.
My all.
Mine.
You.
We.
Us
32

The Sibling Bond

While I was clearly born to be your mother,
I was not born your mother.
It was a role that I morphed into.
Neither of you came with a manual…
It took many years of highs and lows,
trials and errors,
ebbs and flows,
lots of love, patience, comfort, understanding
direction, affection,
teaching and thought expanding.
I was once asked what my greatest
accomplishment was.
I immediately replied, "My children!"
because…
being a mother has been the most satisfying,
and gratifying
role that I have…
or EVER will hold.
In the future, a day will come that there won't be
a tomorrow for me.
Death is a part of life and it's just the way things
are to be.
When that day comes, reach to your side for the
hand of your sister or brother.

You'll be okay. You'll get through it. You'll still
have one another.
Your relationship with each other will surpass
dad and I's time here on earth.
Invest time in each other, be best friends, find
value, appreciation, and worth.
You see, a sibling is the best gift that we ever
could have given you both.
They're a guarantee of a partner, supporter,
encourager for life's decisions and growth.
First turn to God, then to each other to get
through the hardest days.
Trust in God's plan, He has all the answers, got
questions? Simply pray.
I'll be watching from Heaven, protecting and
guiding each of your precious steps.
I'll do this for you and each of your families
until you've taken your final breaths.
A parent's love is forever, here or in Heaven,
you'll be loved until infinity.
Make sure you keep that tight sibling bond-its
what's most important to me!

The Struggle

In the shadows.
In the light.
Shining bright.
Dark midnight.
Dance the thoughts within my mind.

Grab them tight.
Hold them dear.
Once they take flight,
they're in the rear.
Fleeting thoughts get left behind.

Incomplete thoughts.
Weak Recollection.
Anxious movements.
Baited breaths and inflection.
Hopefully, they can't see!

Can't hold this thought.
Over speak.
Cut them off!
Words seep and leak.
Welcome to my ADHD!

My Family

Indescribable.
Tight.
My Comfort.
Beloved.
Caring.
Loving.
Kind.
Happy.
Bonded.
Harmonious.
Influential.
Loved.
Helpful.
Love.
Pleasant.
Attractive.
Respectful.
God-fearing.
Successful.
Passionate.
Supportive.
Talented.
Close.
Valued.
My heart.
Everything.

I Told You

I told you not to expect anything profound.
I wasn't going to share my views on the current
political climate,
or explore the moral complexities of modern
ethical dilemmas.
Explain why the CROWN Act is necessary.
That may have required emotional introspection
or YOUR part.
Maybe on MY part as well.
And I didn't want to think too hard.
I didn't want to expand on my emotional
sobriety or the sacred lessons of the
transformative dissolving ego.
Too deep.
Did you expect to hear me explain why the
Millennials, Gen Z and Gen Alpha are the
beacons of hope for the future?
I told you I wasn't that deep.
I dine alone in an atmosphere of loneliness and
spoon-feed you the superficial dessert.
I told you not to expect
anything other than
what you expect to expect.
Maybe these are just delusions of grandeur?

www.ingramcontent.com/pod-product-compliance
Lightning Source LLC
LaVergne TN
LVHW041254200726